Place value, ordering and rounding

PV1.1 Reading and writing big numbers

TB pages 5–6

A1 Paired activity

B1
Pluto	2300	two thousand three hundred
Mercury	4880	four thousand eight hundred and eighty
Mars	6790	six thousand seven hundred and ninety
Venus	12 100	twelve thousand one hundred
Earth	12 760	twelve thousand seven hundred and sixty
Neptune	49 500	forty-nine thousand five hundred
Uranus	51 000	fifty-one thousand
Saturn	119 990	one hundred and nineteen thousand nine hundred and ninety
Jupiter	142 800	one hundred and forty-two thousand eight hundred

PV1.2 Generating numbers

TB pages 7–8

A1 a 9 765 321, 1 235 679
    b 8 754 320, 2 034 578
    c 8 654 100, 1 004 568

A2 1000, 1998, 2996, 3994, 4992, 5990
    5000, 5998, 6996, 7994, 8992, 9990
    10 000, 10 998, 11 996, 12 994, 13 992, 14 990
    19 000, 19 998, 20 996, 21 994, 22 992, 23 990

B1 a 100   b 1000   c 1
    d 10 000   e 10

B2 a 1000   b 10   c 7
    d 200   e 10 000

B3 CM 1

C1 True
    140 000, 131 000, 122 000, 113 000, 104 000,
    230 000, 221 000, 212 000, 203 000,
    320 000, 311 000, 302 000,
    410 000, 401 000, 500 000

C2 Subtract
    same as
    which is 100 less than …

CM 1

1 a 41 538 −   8 = 41 530
           −   30 = 41 500
           − 500 = 41 000
           − 1000 = 40 000
           − 40 000 =   0

   b 72 614 −   4 = 72 610
           −   10 = 72 600
           − 600 = 72 000
           − 2000 = 70 000
           − 70 000 =   0

   c 576 029 −   9 = 576 020
            −   20 = 576 000
            − 6000 = 570 000
            − 70 000 = 500 000
            − 500 000 =   0

   d 850 485 −   5 = 850 480
            −   80 = 850 400
            − 400 = 850 000
            − 50 000 = 800 000
            − 800 000 =   0

2 a 56 889 +   1 = 56 890
           +   10 = 56 900
           + 100 = 57 000
           + 3000 = 60 000
           + 40 000 = 100 000

   b 35 376 +   4 = 35 380
           +   20 = 35 400
           + 600 = 36 000
           + 4000 = 40 000
           + 60 000 = 100 000

3 a 71 248 +   2 = 71 250
           +   50 = 71 300
           + 4000 = 75 300
           + 10 000 = 85 300

   b 32 514 +   6 = 32 520
           +   30 = 32 550
           + 200 = 32 750
           + 5000 = 37 750
           + 10 000 = 47 750

PV1.3 Ordering large numbers

TB page 9

A1 a 8924, 9482, 11 428, 15 824, 18 248, 108 592
    b 108 592, 18 248, 15 824, 11 428, 9482, 8924

A2 a 14 200 < 14 212
    b 10 216 > 10 026
    c 27 257 < 28 257
    d 36 558 < 46 558
    e 55 005 > 50 050
    f 31 427 > 31 425

B1 a true   b true
    c true   d false

B2 a 17 800   b 26 600
    c 33 800   d 42 756

B3 Children write 5 statements with the middle number:
    a between 14 270 and 14 520
    b between 25 840 and 25 740

B4 a −8, −6, −5, −2, −1, 0, 5
    b −9, −7, −4, −3, 2, 3

PV1.4 Above and below zero

TB pages 10–11

A1 2, 1, 0, −1, −2, −3, −4

A2 a 4, 1, −2, −5, −8, −11, −14
    b 6, 2, −2, −6, −10, −14, −18
    c 5, 0, −5, −10, −15, −20, −25
    d 23, 13, 3, −7, −17, −27, −37

A3

City	Monday	Tuesday	Wednesday	Thursday	Friday
London	5°C	6°C	10°C	13°C	4°C
Toronto	−5°C	−8°C	−6°C	−2°C	−9°C

B1 a 8, 5, 2, −1, −4, −7
    b 22, 13, 4, −5, −14, −23
    c −21, −18, −15, −12, −9, −6
    d 9, 6, 3, 0, −3, −6, −9

B2 a −4°C < 4°C
    b 2°C > −3°C
    c −12°C < −3°C
    d −6°C < 0°C

B3 Monday 10°C, Tuesday 14°C, Wednesday 16°C, Thursday 15°C, Friday 13°C

B4 Toronto −16°C, London 12°C

B5 28°C

C1 Press C 5 − − = 0
    Press C 6 − − = 0
    Press C 7 − − = 0

Children choose their own starting number and record 10 numbers in each sequence.

C2

Start at 20°C	Subtract	Number of steps	Finish at −20°C
	2	20	
	4	10	
	5	8	
	10	4	
	20	2	

The number of steps times the amount you subtract always equals 40.
or
To find the number of steps, divide 20 by the number you subtract and then double your answer.

PV2.1 Estimating quantities and proportions

TB pages 12–13

A1 Accept sensible estimates.
    a $\frac{1}{3}$ full   b $\frac{3}{4}$ full
    c $\frac{1}{5}$ full   d $\frac{1}{4}$ full

A2 a Unlikely to be true.
    b Likely to be true.
    c Most unlikely to be true.
    d Likely to be true.

B1 The following are the measured values for real coins. You will probably use plastic coins, and will need to check that they are the correct sizes.

Value of coin	30 cm	1 m
1p	15	50
2p	11–12	38–39
5p	16–17	55–56
10p	12	40
£1	13	43–44

Real coins vary slightly, so allow close approximations.

B2 a The following are the measured heights of stacks of 10 real coins. Plastic coins may differ.

    1p   1.8 cm
    2p   2.2 cm
    5p   1.8 cm
    10p   1.9 cm
    £1   3.2 cm

    b 10 times the measurement given for a.

C1 There are $40\frac{1}{2}$ bricks in 1 square metre of wall.

C2 a 81 bricks   b 162 bricks
    c $364\frac{1}{2}$ bricks   d 324 bricks
    e 729 bricks   f 1215 bricks

PV2.2 Estimating and rounding 4-digit numbers

TB pages 14–15

A1

number	nearest 10	nearest 100	nearest 1000
4217	4220	4200	4000
4683	4680	4700	5000
5325	5330	5300	5000
5754	5750	5800	6000

A2 Accept close estimates.
    a 500   b 900
    c 0.2   d 0.5
    e −4   f −2
    g −7   h −1

B1 a 604, best approximation 500 + 100
    b 801, best approximation 700 + 100
    c 456, best approximation 20 × 24
    d 464, best approximation 30 × 16

B2 a 437 to the nearest 10 is **440**.
    b 1785 to the nearest 100 is **1800**.
    c 3046 to the nearest 1000 is **3000**.
    d 969 to the nearest 1000 is **1000**.

B3 a Great white shark
    b Sperm whale
    c Blue whale
    d Narwhal
    e Great white shark, killer whale or minke whale
    f Sperm whale

C1

Palindromic number	Rounded to the nearest 10	100	1000
5005	5010	5000	5000
5115	5120	5100	5000
5225	5230	5200	5000
5335	5340	5300	5000
5445	5450	5400	5000
5555	5560	5600	6000
5665	5670	5700	6000
5775	5780	5800	6000
5885	5890	5900	6000
5995	6000	6000	6000

The numbers go up in steps of 110, and so do the numbers rounded to the nearest 10. The numbers rounded to the nearest 100 go up in steps of 100 with a step of 200 in the middle.

To the nearest 1000, the numbers round to 5000 until 5555 and all higher numbers, which round to 6000.

9009	9010	9000	9000
9119	9120	9100	9000
9229	9230	9200	9000
9339	9340	9300	9000
9449	9450	9400	9000
9559	9560	9600	10 000
9669	9670	9700	10 000
9779	9780	9800	10 000
9889	9890	9900	10 000
9999	10 000	10 000	10 000

PV2.3 Estimating and rounding measurements

TB page 16

A1 AB ≈ 5 cm
    CD ≈ 7 cm
    EF ≈ 5 cm
    GH ≈ 9 cm
    IJ ≈ 4 cm
    KL ≈ 10 cm
    MN ≈ 8 cm

B1 a, b Children draw and measure 10 lines.
    c On each line, the parts between 2 adjacent printed lines are the same length.

C1 a 134 mm   b 13 cm
    c 3 cm + 6 cm + 5 cm = 14 cm

d   You get different answers when you round the lengths before you add them and when you add first and round the total.

C2 a   438 mm
    b   44 cm
    c   15 cm + 15 cm + 15 cm = 45 cm
    d   The answers to b and c are different.

CM 4

mountain	height in metres	rounded to nearest		
		10 m	100 m	1000 m
McKinley	6194	6190	6200	6000
Logan	6050	6050	6100	6000
Dawson	3390	3390	3400	3000
Moose Peak	2292	2290	2300	2000
Grouse	1718	1720	1700	2000
Edith Cavell	3363	3360	3400	3000
Robson	3954	3950	4000	4000
Cariboo	1933	1930	1900	2000
Alberta	3619	3620	3600	4000
Columbia	3747	3750	3700	4000

PV3.1 Multiplying by 10 and 100

TB page 17

A1 a   40 × 10 = 400
        400 × 10 = **4000**
        40 × 100 = **4000**

    b   70 × 10 = 700
        700 × 10 = 7000
        70 × 100 = 7000

    c   62 × 10 = 620
        620 × 10 = 6200
        62 × 100 = 6200

    d   34 × 10 = 340
        340 × 10 = 3400
        34 × 100 = 3400

A2 a   4 × 100 = **400**
        40 × 100 = **4000**
        400 × 100 = **40 000**

    b   6 × 100 = **600**
        60 × 100 = **6000**
        600 × 100 = **60 000**

    c   **12** × 100 = 1200
        120 × **100** = 12 000
        1200 × 100 = **120 000**

B1 a   16 160 1600 **16 000** **160 000**
        1 600 000
    b   1.8 18 **180** 1800 **18 000** **180 000**
    c   0.9 **9** 90 900 **9000** **90 000**
    d   Make up own

B2 picture   £205 × 100 = £20 500
    vase   £7.25 × 100 = £725
    chair   £9.50 × 100 = £950
    table   £13.95 × 100 = £1395
    lamp   £4.99 × 100 = £499
    china   £30.70 × 100 = £3070

PV3.2 Dividing by 100

TB page 18

A1 a   21 000
        21 000 ÷ 10 = 2100
        21 000 ÷ 100 = 210

    b   31 500
        31 500 ÷ 10 = 3150
        31 500 ÷ 100 = 315

    c   40 700
        40 700 ÷ 10 = 4070
        40 700 ÷ 100 = 407

A2 a   600 ÷ 100 = **6**
        6000 ÷ 100 = **60**
        60 000 ÷ 100 = **600**

    b   900 ÷ **100** = 9
        9000 ÷ **100** = 90
        90 000 ÷ 100 = 900

A3 a   7000 ÷ 100 = **70**
    b   4600 ÷ 100 = **46**
    c   13 000 ÷ 100 = **130**
    d   53 000 ÷ 100 = **530**

B1 a   400 000 ÷ 100 = 4000
        40 000 ÷ 100 = **400**
        4000 ÷ 100 = **40**
        400 ÷ 100 = **4**
        40 ÷ 100 = **0.4**

    b   600 000 ÷ 100 = 6000
        60 000 ÷ 100 = 600
        6000 ÷ 100 = 60
        600 ÷ 100 = 6
        60 ÷ 100 = 0.6

    c   120 000 ÷ 100 = 1200
        12 000 ÷ 100 = 120
        1200 ÷ 100 = 12
        120 ÷ 100 = 1.2
        12 ÷ 100 = 0.12

d   390 000 ÷ 100 = 3900
    39 000 ÷ 100 = 390
    3900 ÷ 100 = 39
    390 ÷ 100 = 3.9
    39 ÷ 100 = 0.39

B2 £250 is 25 £10 notes, 250 £1 coins, 2500 10p coins, 25 000 1p coins.

B3 CM 7

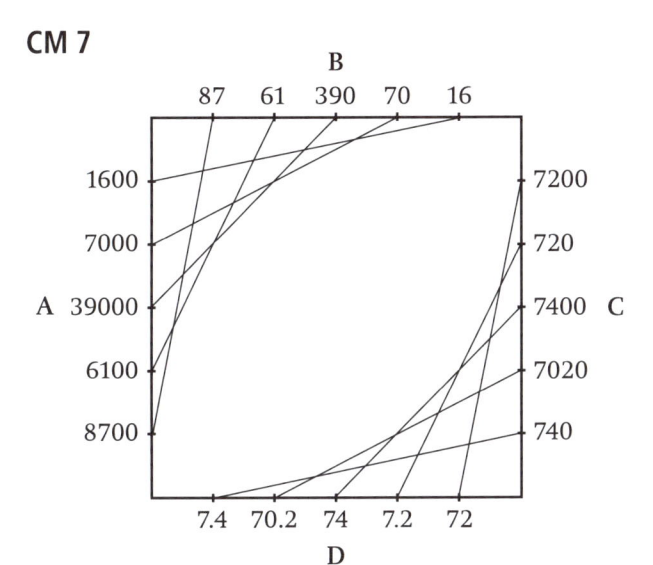

CM 7

```
            B
      87  61  390  70  16
   1600                        7200
   7000                         720
A  39000                       7400  C
   6100                        7020
   8700                         740
      7.4 70.2 74 7.2 72
            D
```

CM 8

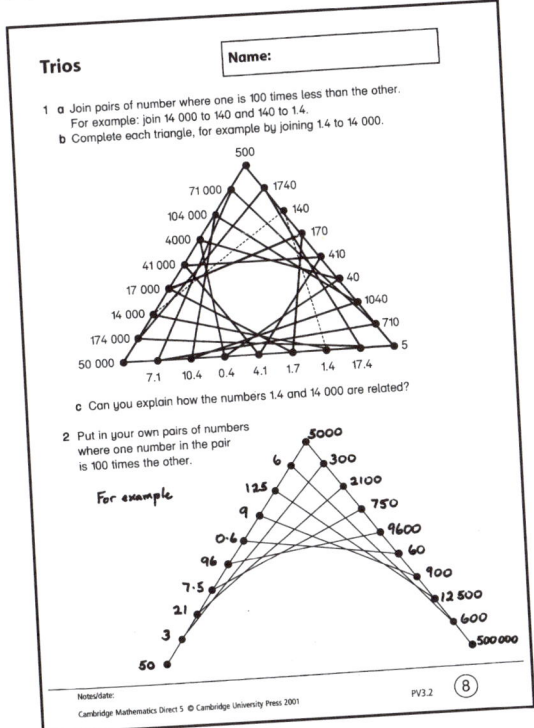

(Worksheet "Trios" — Cambridge Mathematics Direct 5 © Cambridge University Press 2001, PV3.2, page 8)

PV3.3 Using a calculator for multiplication and division

TB page 19

A1 a [47] × 100 [**4700**] × 10 [47 000] ÷ 10 [4700] ÷ 100 [**47**]
    b [39] × 10 [**390**] × 100 [**39 000**] ÷ 100 [**390**] ÷ 10 [**39**]
    c [65] × 100 [**6500**] × 10 [**65 000**] ÷ 100 [**650**] ÷ 10 [**65**]
    d [80] × 10 [**800**] × 100 [**80 000**] ÷ 10 [**8000**] ÷ 100 [**80**]

A2 The first and last number in each track are the same.

A3 CM 9

B1 a [16] × 10 [160] + 10 [170]
       [16] + 10 [26] × 10 [260]
       [16] × 100 [1600] + 10 [1610]
       [16] + 10 [26] × 100 [2600]

    b [23] × 10 [230] + 10 [240]
       [23] + 10 [33] × 10 [330]
       [23] × 100 [2300] + 10 [2310]
       [23] + 10 [33] × 100 [3300]
       [39] × 10 [390] + 10 [400]
       [39] + 10 [49] × 10 [490]
       [39] × 100 [3900] + 10 [3910]
       [39] + 10 [49] × 100 [4900]

    c There is always a difference of 90 between the numbers at the end of track A and of 990 between those at the end of track B.

B2 a [16] × 10 [160] × 10 [1600] + 10 [1610]
       [16] + 10 [26] × 10 [260] × 10 [2600]
       [23] × 10 [230] × 10 [2300] + 10 [2310]
       [23] + 10 [33] × 10 [330] × 10 [3300]
       [39] × 10 [390] × 10 [3900] + 10 [3910]
       [39] + 10 [49] × 10 [490] × 10 [4900]

    b Tracks B and C give the same end numbers because × 100 is the same as × 10 × 10

B3 [100] × 10 [1000] + 10 [1010]
    [100] + 10 [110] × 10 [1100]
    [100] × 100 [10 000] + 10 [10 010]
    [100] + 10 [110] × 100 [11 000]
    [100] × 10 [1000] × 10 [10 000] + 10 [10 010]
    [100] + 10 [110] × 10 [1100] × 10 [11 000]

C1 Children's tracks starting with 3- and 4-digit numbers.

Properties of numbers and number sequences

N1.1 Square numbers 1

Pupil activities 2

square side 1 cm → 1 square cm
square side 2 cm → 4 square cm
square side 3 cm → 9 square cm
square side 4 cm → 16 square cm
   4 squares in a row, 4 rows
   → 4 + 4 + 4 + 4 = 4 × 4
square side 5 cm → 25 square cm
   5 squares in a row, 5 rows
   → 5 + 5 + 5 + 5 + 5 = 5 × 5
square side 6 cm → 36 square cm
   6 squares in a row, 6 rows
   → 6 + 6 + 6 + 6 + 6 + 6 = 6 × 6
square side 7 cm → 49 square cm
   7 squares in a row, 7 rows
   → 7 + 7 + 7 + 7 + 7 + 7 + 7 = 7 × 7
square side 8 cm → 64 square cm
   8 squares in a row, 8 rows
   → 8 + 8 + 8 + 8 + 8 + 8 + 8 + 8 = 8 × 8
square side 9 cm → 81 square cm
   9 squares in a row, 9 rows
   → 9 + 9 + 9 + 9 + 9 + 9 + 9 + 9 + 9 = 9 × 9
square side 10 cm → 100 square cm
   10 squares in a row, 10 rows
   → 10 + 10 + 10 + 10 + 10 + 10 + 10 + 10 + 10 + 10 = 10 × 10

N1.2 Square numbers 2

TB pages 20–21

A1   a, b

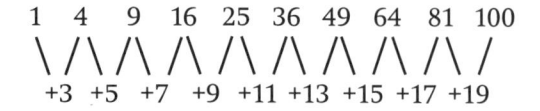

1 4 9 16 25 36 49 64 81 100
+3 +5 +7 +9 +11 +13 +15 +17 +19

    c The differences go up by 2. The difference between any consecutive pair of square numbers is 2 more than the difference between the pair before it.
    or The difference between consecutive square numbers increases in the pattern of odd numbers.
    d 121

A2   a 3 counters in each row
       b 9 is the square of 3.

A3   a 4   b 2   c 6
      d 10   e 5   f 7

B1   a 9   b 4   c 64   d 25
      e 100 f 81   g 1   h 49

B2   a You can get from one square to the next by adding little squares on 2 sides. The number of little squares added is twice the number in the side of the last square, plus 1.
In the first column of numbers, you add on the number that is 2 more than the last number you added on. The numbers you are adding are consecutive odd numbers starting with 1. The number of numbers is equal to the number of little squares in the side of the big square.

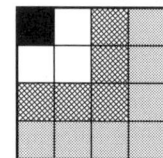

    b

$1 + 3 + 5 + 7 = 16 = 4 \times 4 = 4^2$

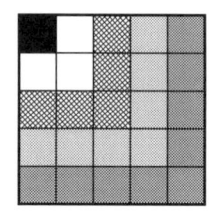

$1 + 3 + 5 + 7 + 9 = 25 = 5 \times 5 = 5^2$

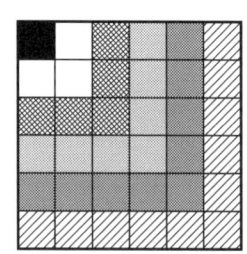

$1 + 3 + 5 + 7 + 9 + 11 = 36 = 6 \times 6 = 6^2$

    c 100. We can see this from the pattern. The sum of the first 10 odd numbers is the square of 10.

C1   a Each row is 2 squares longer than the row above. The first row is 1 square, and the number of squares in any shape is the sum of consecutive odd numbers.
       b The number of squares in each shape is a square number / is the square of the number of rows.

c

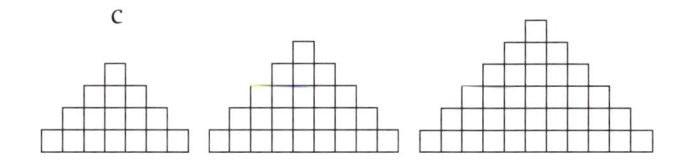

d   Cut a section with a vertical line on one side of the top square, and move the section to the other side:

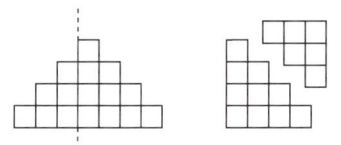

CM 10

Number of rows	Number of little squares	Difference
1	1	
2	4	3
3	9	5
4	16	7
5	25	9
6	36	11
7	49	13

CM 11

$1 \to 1^2$
$4 \to$ the square of 2
$9 \to 3^2$
$16 \to 4$ squared
$25 \to 5^2$
$36 \to 6 \times 6$
$49 \to 7^2$
eighty-one $\to 9^2$
$10^2 \to 10 \times 10$

N1.3 Odd and even numbers

TB page 22

A1 a   3 of: 16, 18, 20, 22, 24
    b   Answers will all be even.
    c   The totals are all even.
    d   4 even numbers greater than 15 and their sum. The sum is even.
    e   Sum of 2 more sets of 4 even numbers. The totals are all even.
    f   The sum of even numbers is even.

A2 a   1 of:
        100 − 57 = 43
        100 − 37 = 63
        100 − 13 = 87
        100 − 5 = 95
        57 − 24 = 33
        57 − 20 = 37
        37 − 24 = 13
        37 − 20 = 17
        24 − 13 = 11
        24 − 5 = 19
        20 − 13 = 7
        20 − 5 = 15
    b   Another difference from the list in a
    c   The difference between an odd and an even number is odd.
    d   1 of:
        57 − 37 = 20
        57 − 13 = 44
        57 − 5 = 52
        37 − 13 = 24
        37 − 5 = 32
        13 − 5 = 8
    e   Another difference from the list in d
    f   The difference between 2 odd numbers is even.

C1 3 = 1 + 2
    5 = 2 + 3
    6 = 1 + 2 + 3
    7 = 3 + 4
    9 = 4 + 5 or 2 + 3 + 4
    10 = 1 + 2 + 3 + 4
    11 = 5 + 6
    12 = 3 + 4 + 5
    13 = 6 + 7
    14 = 2 + 3 + 4 + 5
    15 = 7 + 8 or 1 + 2 + 3 + 4 + 5 or 4 + 5 + 6
    17 = 8 + 9
    18 = 3 + 4 + 5 + 6 or 5 + 6 + 7
    19 = 9 + 10
    20 = 2 + 3 + 4 + 5 + 6

You can't make 1, 2, 4, 8 or 16 by adding consecutive numbers.

CM 12

2   If you add 3 odd numbers together, the answer will be odd.

3   If you add 4 odd numbers together, the answer will be even.

4   If you add 4 even numbers together, the answer will be even.

N1.4 Counting on and back

CM 13

1. 0, 6, 12, 18, 24, 30, 36, 42, 48, 54, 60, 66, 72, 78
   For example: The circled numbers are in 3 columns starting with 0, 6 and 12, with numbers in alternate rows circled. The units digits follow the pattern 0, 6, 2, 8, 4, 0, …

2. 3, 9, 15, 21, 27, 33, 39, 45, 51, 57, 63, 69, 75
   For example: As in 1, the circled numbers are in 3 columns, with numbers in alternate rows circled. The units digits follow a similar pattern, 3, 9, 5, 1, 7, 3, …

3. 0, 8, 16, 24, 32, 40, 48, 56, 64, 72, 80, 88, 96
   For example: The circled numbers are on lines sloping down and left from 8, 48 and 88. Each circle is 1 row down and 2 columns to the left of the circle before. The units digits follow the patern 0, 8, 6, 4, 2, 0, …

4. 5, 13, 21, 29, 37, 45, 53, 61, 69, 77, 85, 93
   For example: The pattern is formed in the same way, by adding 8. Because we started with a different number the pattern is moved sideways.

CM 14

1. −12, −9, −6, 3, 0, 3, 6, 9, 12

2. 121, 118, 115, 112, 109, 106, 103, 100, 97, 94, 91, 88, 85, 82, 79, 76, 73, 70, 67, 64, 61, 58, 55, 52, 49, 46, 43, 40, 37, 34, 31, 28, 25, 22, 19, 16, 13, 10, 7, 4, 1

3. 0, 9, 18, 27, 36, 45, 54, 63, 72, 81, 90, 99
   If you continued the pattern 127 would not be circled because it does not lie on the diagonal sloping down from 99.

4. 7, 14, 21, 28, 35, 42, 49, 56, 63, 70, 77, 84, 91, 98
   If you continued the pattern 135 would not be circled because it lies between the lines sloping down from 91 and from 84.

N1.5 Divisibility

TB page 23

B1 500, 8700, 31 000, 64 900

B2 a, b, c

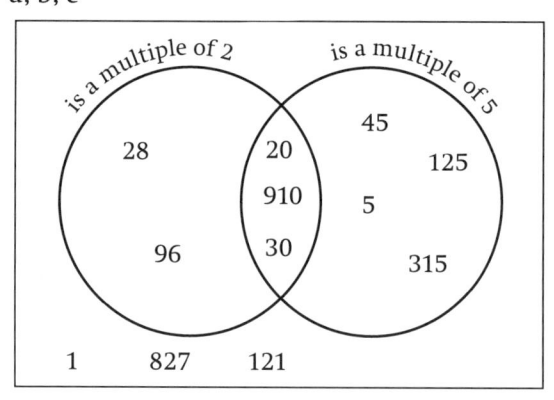

d   For example: The numbers that are multiples of both 2 and 5 are multiples of 10, … all end in 0.
e   Numbers that are multiples of 100 are multiples of both 2 and 5, so go in the overlap.
f   Multiples of 20 would also go in the overlap because they are also multiples of both 2 and 5.

CM 15

1. Numbers circled in red: 160, 80, 546, 120, 180, 186, 650, 174, 88, 348, 98
   Numbers circled in blue: 160, 25, 80, 120, 180, 650, 135
   Numbers circled in green: 160, 80, 120, 180, 650

2. All the numbers circled in red and blue are also circled in green.

3. Numbers divisible by 100: 900, 1200, 3500, 7000

N2.1 Sequences and patterns

TB pages 24–25

A1 a 7 14 21 **28 35 42 49 56 63** 70
    b 6 12 **18** 24 30 36 **42 48 54** 60
    c 15 10 5 0 **−5 −10 −15 −20 −25** −30
    d −48 **−40 −32 −24 −16 −8** 0 8 16 24
    e −63 **−54 −45 −36 −27 −18 −9** 0 9 18

A2 Children's pattern, both drawn and described

B1 a 4 7 10 **13 16 19 22**
       Rule: add 3 each time.
    b 7 12 17 **22 27 32 37**
       Rule: add 5 each time.
    c 48 39 30 **21 12 3 −6**
       Rule: take away 9 each time.

d 16 9 2 −5 −12 −19 −26
Rule: take away 7 each time.
e −23 −29 −35 −41 −47 −53 −59
Rule: take away 6 each time.
f −65 −57 −49 −41 −33 −25 −17
Rule: add 8 each time.

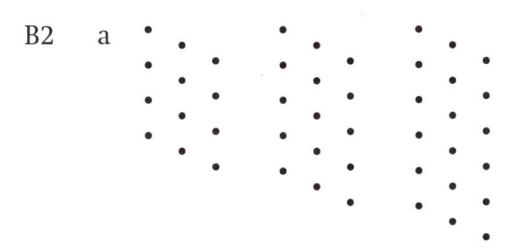

B2 a

The rule is: Add another diagonal of 3 each time.

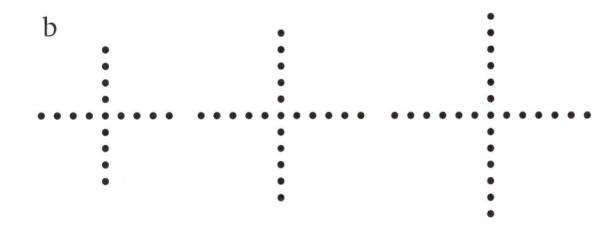

b

The rule is: Add 4 more each time, 1 at the end of each arm

C1 a 30 in the 10th pattern. 300 in the 100th pattern.
    b 41 in the 10th pattern. 401 in the 100th pattern.

C2 Children make up their own pattern and work out how many are in the 10th and 100th diagrams.

N2.2 Sequences with 2-digit steps

TB pages 26–27

A1 CM 16
A2 a 1 12 23 **34 45 56**
    b 13 26 39 **52 65 78**
    c 100 89 78 **67 56 45**
    d 145 130 115 **100 85 70**
A3 a 110   b 63   c 57   d 200
B1 a 100 121 142 163 **184 205 226 247**
       The rule is add 21 each time.
    b 200 185 170 155 **140 125 110 95**
       The rule is take away 15 each time.
    c 1 3 6 10 **15 21 28 36**
       The rule is add 2, then 3, then 4 and so on.
    d 1 4 9 16 **25 36 49 64**
       The rule is add 3, then 5, then 7 and so on (or write down the next square number).

e −105 −84 −63 **−42 −21 0 21**
   The rule is add 21.
B2 7 28 **49 70 91 112 133**
B3 19 38 **57 76 95 114 133**
C1 16 32 48 64 80 96 112 128 144
C2 12 24 36 48 60 72 84 96 108 120
    132 144
    You must press = 12 times to reach 144.
    This is because 12 × 12 = 144 and
    9 × 16 = 144
C3 a 15 30 45 **60 75 90**
    b 18 36 54 **72 90**
C4 a 15 30 45 60 **75** 90 105 120 135
       150 165 180 195 210 **225** 240 255
       270 285 **300**

       25 50 **75** 100 125 **150** 175 200
       225 250 275 **300**

    b

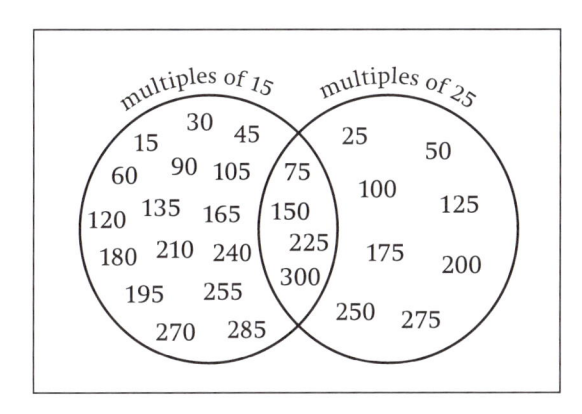

[Venn diagram: multiples of 15 and multiples of 25]
multiples of 15: 15, 30, 45, 60, 90, 105, 120, 135, 165, 180, 210, 240, 195, 255, 270, 285
Intersection: 75, 150, 225, 300
multiples of 25: 25, 50, 100, 125, 175, 200, 250, 275

CM 16

1 a 225 and 75, 125 and 200, and 250, 175 and 150 are coloured red.
   b 25 50 **75** 100 **125 150 175
      200** 275 250
   c The rule is: add **25** each time.
2 a 21 42 63 **84 105 126 147 168
      189 210**
   b 126 and 210, 105 and 147, 84 and 168 are coloured blue.
   c The rule is: **add 21** each time.
3 a **12** 24 36 48 60 72 84 96
      108 120
   b The difference is 12.
   c The rule is: **add 12** each time.

Homework suggestion

2 23 44 65 86 107 128 149 170 191
5 26 47 68 89 110 131 152 173 194
7 28 49 70 91 112 133 154 175 196

12 24 36 48 60 72 84
14 28 42 56 70 84

15 30 45 60 75 90
18 36 54 72 90

12 24 36 48 60 72 84
21 42 63 84

N2.3 Multiples and factors

TB pages 28–29

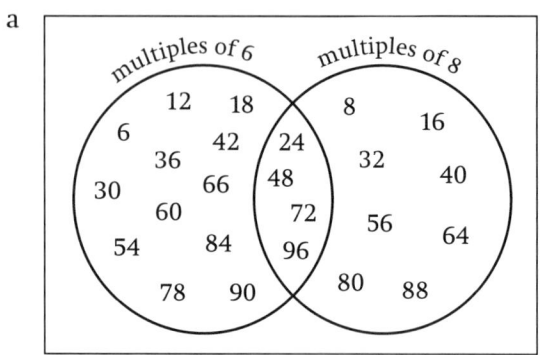

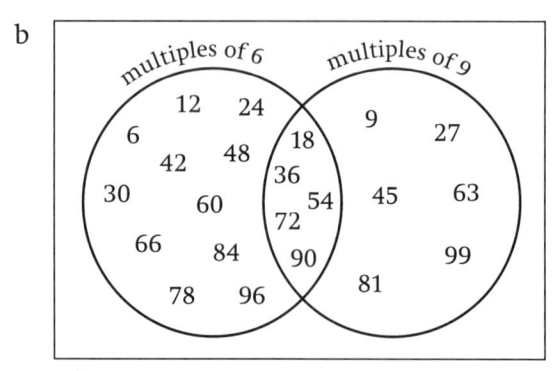

A1 a *multiples of 6*: 12, 18, 6, 42, 36, 30, 66, 60, 54, 84, 78, 90
intersection: 24, 48, 72, 96
multiples of 8: 8, 16, 32, 40, 56, 64, 80, 88

b *multiples of 6*: 12, 24, 6, 42, 48, 30, 60, 66, 84, 78, 96
intersection: 18, 36, 54, 72, 90
multiples of 9: 9, 27, 45, 63, 99, 81

A2 a $48 \div 8 = 6$ $48 \div 8 = 6$
Missing factor 6.
b $63 \div 9 = 7$ $63 \div 7 = 9$
Missing factor 7.
c $77 \div 11 = 7$ $77 \div 7 = 11$
Missing product 77.
d $54 \div 9 = 6$ $54 \div 6 = 9$
Missing product 54.
e $88 \div 11 = 8$ $88 \div 8 = 11$
Missing product 88.
f $35 \div 7 = 5$ $35 \div 5 = 7$
Missing factor 5.
g $72 \div 9 = 8$ $72 \div 8 = 9$
Missing factor 8.
h $56 \div 8 = 7$ $56 \div 7 = 8$
Missing product 56.

B1 a 4 red, 3 white, 4 red, 3 white, ...
b The 23rd counter is red.
c The 54th counter is white.
d The 25th red counter is the 43rd counter.
e The 25th white counter is the 61st counter.

B2 a 3 red, 2 white, 3 blue, ...
b The 23rd counter is blue.
c The 54th counter is blue.
d The 25th red counter is the 65th counter.
e The 25th white counter is the 100th counter.

C1 a Children's calculation with their chosen 2-digit number
b 5 more calculations with 2-digit numbers.
The number you end up with is the digital sum of the number you started with.
c It doesn't work with 3-digit numbers.

CM 17

CM 18

1 a 72, 180, 54, 240, 180
   b 63, 180, 270
   c 49, 56, 630, 140
   d 121, 110, 77, 99, 198, 132

2 Children's own puzzle

3 a 76, 57, 190, 133, 95, 570, 209, 380
   b 105, 210, 63, 126, 84, 231, 420

N2.4 Pairs of factors

TB pages 30–31

A1

×	1	2	3	4	5
1	1	2	3	4	5
2	2	4	6	8	10
3	3	6	9	(12)	15
4	4	8	(12)	16	20
5	5	10	15	20	25

A2 a 12   b 24   c 36   d 40

A3 a The factors of 12 are **1 and 12**, 2 and 6, 3 and 4.
    b The factors of 24 are **1 and 24, 2 and 12**, 3 and 8, 4 and 6.
    c The factors of 36 are **1 and 36, 2 and 18, 3 and 12**, 4 and 9, 6 and 6.
    d The factors of 40 are **1 and 40, 2 and 20**, 4 and 10, 5 and 8.

B1 a 1 and 20, 2 and 10, 4 and 5
    b 1 and 35, 5 and 7
    c 1 and 48, 2 and 24, 3 and 16, 4 and 12, 6 and 8
    d 1 and 54, 2 and 27, 3 and 18, 6 and 9
    e 1 and 60, 2 and 30, 3 and 20, 4 and 15, 5 and 12, 6 and 10
    f 1 and 75, 3 and 25, 5 and 15
    g 1 and 90, 2 and 45, 3 and 30, 5 and 18, 6 and 15, 9 and 10
    h 1 and 98, 2 and 49, 7 and 14

B2 Each answer can be calculated in a number of different ways using factors. The following are possible examples:
   a 18 × 12 = 2 × 9 × 12 = 2 × 108 = 216
          = 3 × 6 × 12 = 3 × 72 = 216
          = 18 × 3 × 2 × 2 = 54 × 2 × 2 =
          108 × 2 = 216
   b 16 × 14 = 2 × 2 × 2 × 2 × 14
          = 2 × 2 × 2 × 28 = 2 × 2 × 56
          = 2 × 112 = 224
          = 16 × 7 × 2 = 112 × 2 = 224
   c See C1a below.
   d 15 × 18 = 3 × 5 × 2 × 9 = 10 × 27 = 270
          = 15 × 2 × 9 = 30 × 9 = 270
          = 3 × 5 × 18 = 3 × 90 = 270
   e 17 × 12 = 17 × 3 × 2 × 2 = 51 × 2 × 2
          = 102 × 2 = 204
   f 22 × 15 = 2 × 11 × 3 × 5 = 33 × 10 = 330
          = 11 × 2 × 15 = 11 × 30 = 330

C1 a (15 × 2) × 8 = 30 × 8 = 240
       3 × (5 × 2) × 8 = 3 × 10 × 8 = 24 × 10 = 240
       3 × (5 × 8) × 2 = 3 × 40 × 2 = 120 × 2 = 240
       3 × (5 × 4) × 4 = 3 × 20 × 4 = 12 × 20 = 240
       (15 × 2) × 2 × 2 × 2 = 30 × 2 × 2 × 2
          = 60 × 2 × 2 = 120 × 2 = 240
       5 × (3 × 2) × 8 = 5 × 6 × 8 = 30 × 8 = 240
       5 × (3 × 16) = 5 × 48 = 240
       Children state which they like best.
    b Possible methods include the following:
       (12 × 9) × 2 = 108 × 2 = 216
       (12 × 6) × 3 = 72 × 3 = 216
       2 × 2 × (3 × 9) × 2 = 2 × 2 × 27 × 2
          = 2 × 2 × 54 = 2 × 108 = 216
       2 × 2 × (3 × 6) × 3 = 2 × 2 × 18 × 3
          = 2 × 2 × 54 = 2 × 108 = 216
       2 × (6 × 9) × 2 = 2 × 54 × 2 = 2 × 108 = 216
       2 × (6 × 6) × 3 = 2 × 36 × 3 = 2 × 108 = 216
       2 × (6 × 3) × 3 × 2 = 2 × 18 × 3 × 2
          = 2 × 54 × 2 = 2 × 108 = 216
       3 × (4 × 6) × 3 = 3 × 24 × 3 = 3 × 72 = 216
       3 × (4 × 9) × 2 = 3 × 36 × 2 = 3 × 72 = 216
       3 × (4 × 3) × 3 × 2 = 3 × 12 × 3 × 2
          = 3 × 36 × 2 = 3 × 72 = 216
       2 × 2 × (3 × 18) = 2 × 2 × 54 = 2 × 108 = 216

CM 19

1.

Number of factors										
10										
9					36					100
8					18					50
7					12		64			25
6					9		32			20
5				16	6		16		81	10
4				8		4		8	27	5
3		4	9	4	25	3	49	4	9	4
2		2	3	2	5	2	7	2	3	2
1	1	1	1	1	1	1	1	1	1	1
	1	4	9	16	25	36	49	64	81	100

Square numbers

2   a   The square numbers that have an odd number of factors are:
1, 4, 9, 16, 25, 36, 49, 64, 81, 100

b   The square numbers that have an even number of factors are: none

3   a   144: 1, 2, 3, 4, 6, 8, 9, 12, 16, 18, 24, 36, 48, 72, 144   15 factors

b   225: 1, 3, 5, 9, 15, 25, 45, 75, 225   9 factors

c   256: 1, 2, 4, 8, 16, 32, 64, 128, 256   9 factors

d   400: 1, 2, 4, 5, 8, 10, 16, 20, 25, 40, 50, 80, 100, 200, 400   15 factors

4   For example: Square numbers always have an odd number of factors.

Homework suggestion

Numbers with exactly 2 factors: 2, 3, 5, 7, 11, 13, 17, 19, 23

Numbers with more than 4 factors: 12 (1, 2, 3, 4, 6, 12), 16 (1, 2, 4, 8, 16), 18 (1, 2, 3, 6, 9, 18), 20 (1, 2, 4, 5, 10, 20), 24 (1, 2, 3, 4, 6, 8, 12, 24)

N2.5 Multiples of more than 1 number

TB pages 32–33

A1   15, 30, 45

A2   a

multiples of 2	multiples of 4	multiples of 8
2	4	8
4	8	16
6	**12**	24
8	16	**32**
10	20	40
12	**24**	48
14	28	56
16	**32**	64

b   Every 2nd multiple of 2 is a multiple of **4**.
Every 2nd multiple of **4** is a multiple of 8.
Every **4th** multiple of 2 is a multiple of 8.

c   16 = 8 × **2**   32 = 8 × **4**
16 = 4 × **4**   32 = 4 × **8**
16 = 2 × **8**   32 = 2 × **16**

B1   a   21, 42, 63, 84
b   40, 80
c   12, 24, 36, 48, 60, 72, 84, 96
d   18, 36, 54, 72, 90

B2   They are 2-jump, 4-jump and 5-jump crickets.

B3   a   36   b   36   c   84

C1   For example:
a   My number is a multiple of 5 and 7, less than 50, and 1 less than a square number.
b   My number is a multiple of 3, 4 and 6, 1 less than a square number, and less than 50.
c   My number is a multiple of 3 and 9, is 1 more than a multiple of 5, and less than 100.

C2   a   104, 112, 120, 128, 136, 144, 152, 160, 168, 176, 184, 192, 200
b   108, 126, 144, 162, 180, 198
c   120, 150, 180

CM 20

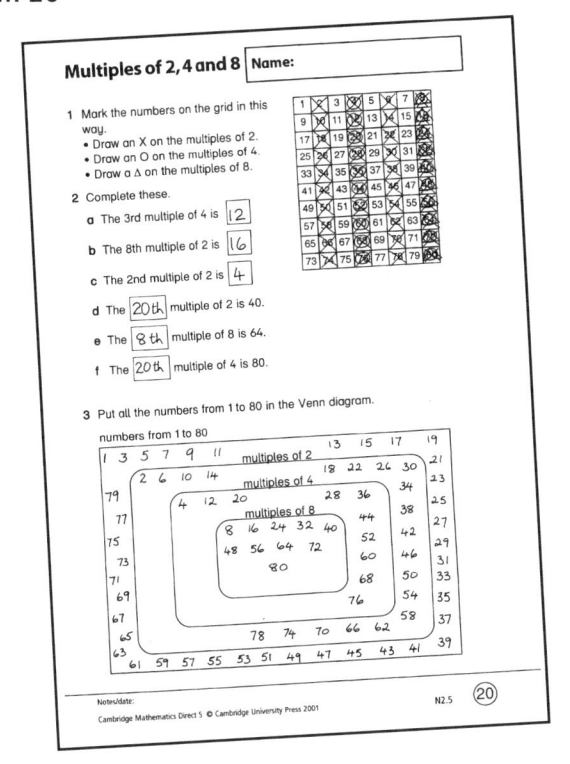

[Worksheet image: Multiples of 2, 4 and 8]

1 Mark the numbers on the grid in this way.
 • Draw an X on the multiples of 2.
 • Draw an O on the multiples of 4.
 • Draw a △ on the multiples of 8.

2 Complete these.
 a The 3rd multiple of 4 is 12.
 b The 8th multiple of 2 is 16.
 c The 2nd multiple of 2 is 4.
 d The 20th multiple of 2 is 40.
 e The 8th multiple of 8 is 64.
 f The 20th multiple of 4 is 80.

3 Put all the numbers from 1 to 80 in the Venn diagram.

Homework suggestion

a 9, 15, 21, 27, 33, 39, 45, 51, 57, 63, 69, 75, 81, 87, 93, 99

b 9, 14, 19, 24, 29, 34, 39, 44, 49, 54, 59, 64, 69, 74, 79, 84, 89, 94, 99

N3.1 Making general statements

TB pages 34–35

A1   a, b, c

0	1	2	3	4	5	6	7	8	9
10	11	12	13	14	15	16	17	18	19
20	21	22	23	24	25	26	27	28	29
30	31	32	33	34	35	36	37	38	39
40	41	42	43	44	45	46	47	48	49
50	51	52	53	54	55	56	57	58	59
60	61	62	63	64	65	66	67	68	69
70	71	72	73	74	75	76	77	78	79
80	81	82	83	84	85	86	87	88	89
90	91	92	93	94	95	96	97	98	99

(Circled: 9, 18, 27, 36, 45, 54, 63, 72, 81, 90, 99)

b–e Children choose 4 random numbers from the grid, note whether each is a multiple of 9, and find its digit sum.

A2 Children write their examples for 'Four-in-a-row'.

B1 a 9 × 12 = 108
 9 × 23 = 207
 9 × 34 = 306
 9 × 45 = 405
 9 × 56 = 504
 9 × 67 = 603
 The number multiplied by 9 increases by 11 each time and the answer increases by 99.
 or In the answer the hundreds get 1 greater and the units 1 smaller each time.

 b 12 × 9 = 108
 123 × 9 = 1107
 1234 × 9 = 11 106
 12 345 × 9 = 111 105
 123 456 × 9 = 1 111 104
 1 234 567 × 9 = 11 111 103
 The number multiplied by 9 includes the next consecutive digit, and in the answer the units get 1 smaller and you add a 1 at the beginning each time.

 c 1 × 1089 = 1089
 2 × 1089 = 2178
 3 × 1089 = 3267
 4 × 1089 = 4356
 5 × 1089 = 5445
 6 × 1089 = 6534
 The thousands and hundreds get 1 greater and the tens and units get 1 smaller each time.

B2 a 5 × 9 = 45
 55 × 9 = 495
 555 × 9 = 4995
 You add 9 in the middle each time.

 b 6 × 9 = 54
 66 × 9 = 594
 666 × 9 = 5994
 You add 9 in the middle each time.

 c 9 × 9 = 81
 99 × 9 = 891
 999 × 9 = 8991
 You add 9 in the middle each time.

C1

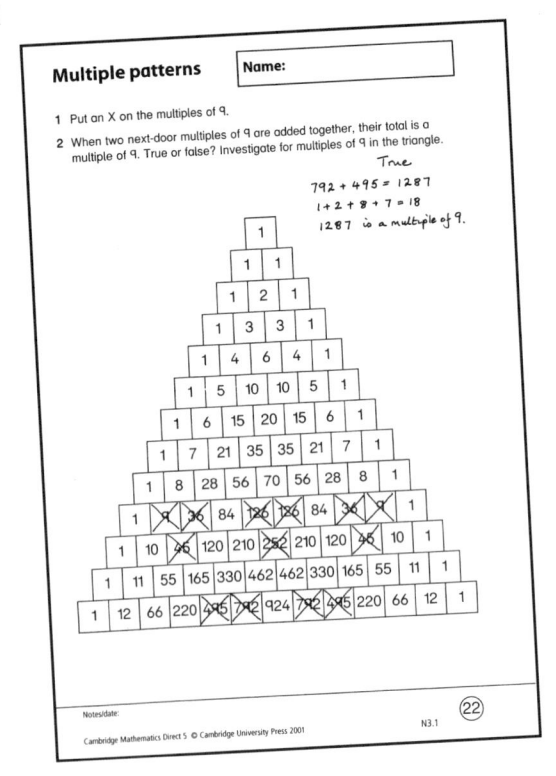

Multiple patterns

1 Put an X on the multiples of 9.
2 When two next-door multiples of 9 are added together, their total is a multiple of 9. True or false? Investigate for multiples of 9 in the triangle.

True
792 + 495 = 1287
1 + 2 + 8 + 7 = 18
1287 is a multiple of 9.

(Pascal's triangle with multiples of 9 marked with X)

Homework suggestion

The multiples of 7 on Pascal's triangle form 2 diagonal lines meeting on the bottom row at 924: 7, 28, 84, 210, 462, 924.

N3.2 Patterns and puzzles

TB pages 36–37

★1 (three diagrams: 3–7–4 / 8–9 / 5; 6 / 13–14 / 7–15–8; 8–17–9 / 18–19 / 10)

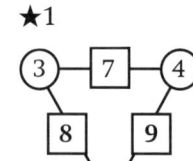

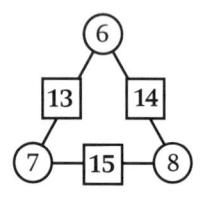

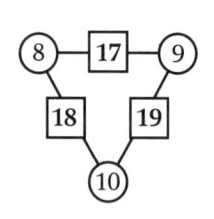

A1 (three diagrams: 15–31–16 / 32–33 / 17; 12 / 26–25 / 14–27–13; 19–39–20 / 40–41 / 21)

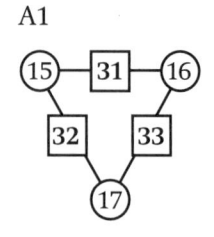

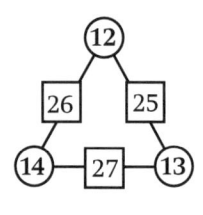

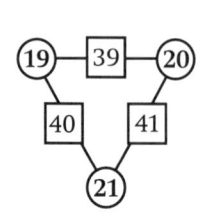

A2 a 4 + 5 + 6 = 15
    b 8 + 9 + 10 = 27
    c 11 + 12 + 13 = 36
    d 19 + 20 + 21 = 60

B1 a 5 and 6   b 7 and 8
    c 8 and 9   d 10 and 11
    e 19 and 20   f 20 and 21
    g 24 and 25   h 32 and 33

B2 a 7 + 8 + 9 = 24
    b 12 + 13 + 14 = 39
    c 15 + 16 + 17 = 48
    d 40 + 41 + 42 = 123
    e 99 + 100 + 101 = 300
    f 53 + 54 + 55 = 162
    g 73 + 74 + 75 = 222
    h 67 + 68 + 69 = 204

B3 a

Multiples of 5	5 consecutive numbers
20	2 + 3 + 4 + 5 + 6
35	5 + 6 + 7 + 8 + 9
80	14 + 15 + 16 + 17 + 18
125	23 + 24 + 25 + 26 + 27

b Children choose 5 more multiples of 5 and add them into the table.

C1 You can write the multiples of 7 (greater than or equal to 28) as the sum of 7 consecutive numbers, e.g.
28 = 1 + 2 + 3 + 4 + 5 + 6 + 7
You can write the multiples of 9 (greater than or equal to 45) as the sum of 9 consecutive numbers, e.g.
81 = 5 + 6 + 7 + 8 + 9 + 10 + 11 + 12 + 13
You can write the multiples of 11 (greater than or equal to 66) as the sum of 11 consecutive numbers, e.g.
99 = 4 + 5 + 6 + 7 + 8 + 9 + 10 + 11 + 12 + 13 + 14

C2 You cannot write 4, 8, 16, 32, 64, … as the sum of consecutive numbers.
You can write 12 as the sum of 3 consecutive numbers: 3 + 4 + 5
You can write 20 as the sum of 5 consecutive numbers: 2 + 3 + 4 + 5 + 6
You can write 24 as the sum of 3 consecutive numbers: 7 + 8 + 9
and so on
You can only write an even number as the sum of consecutive numbers if it is a multiple of an odd number.

N3.3 Factor puzzles

TB pages 38–39

A1 10: 1 × 10
        2 × 5
    11: 1 × 11
    12: 1 × 12
        2 × 6
        3 × 4
    13: 1 × 13

14: 1 × 14
2 × 7
15: 1 × 15
3 × 5
16: 1 × 16
2 × 8
4 × 4
17: 1 × 17
18: 1 × 18
2 × 9
3 × 6
19: 1 × 19
20: 1 × 20
2 × 10
4 × 5

A2

Number of squares	Number of rectangles
1	1
2	1
3	1
4	2
5	1
6	2
7	1
8	2
9	2
10	2
11	1
12	3
13	1
14	2
15	2
16	3
17	1
18	3
19	1
20	3

B1, B2

Squares	Rectangles
3	1
6	2
5	1
10	2
7	1
14	2
9	2
18	3

B3 a When you double the number of squares, you can make 1 more rectangle.

b

Squares	Rectangles
2	1
4	2
4	2
8	2
6	2
12	3
8	2
16	3

It does not work for all even, 1-digit numbers and their doubles.

B4 a

Number of squares	Number of rectangles
21	2
22	2
23	1
24	4
25	2

b 24 squares gives the greatest number of rectangles.
c 24 has more factor pairs than any other number up to 25.

B5 a 36, 48 or 100 squares give exactly 5 rectangles.
b Children draw rectangles:
1 × 36, 2 × 18, 3 × 12, 4 × 9, 6 × 6 or
1 × 48, 2 × 24, 3 × 16, 4 × 12, 6 × 8 or
1 × 100, 2 × 50, 4 × 25, 5 × 20, 10 × 10

B6 You can make 4 rectangles with 40 squares.

C1 a You can make 1 rectangle with 53 squares.
b You can make
1 rectangle with 61 squares,
1 rectangle with 89 squares,
2 rectangles with 169 squares,
2 rectangles with 361 squares,
2 rectangles with 529 squares.

C2 a two of 59, 67, 71, 73, 79, 83, 97
b one of 121, 143, 187

Homework suggestion

You can make 5 rectangles with 100 squares:
1 × 100, 2 × 50, 4 × 25, 5 × 20, 10 × 10

N3.4 Patterns and sequences

TB pages 40–41

A1 a
+2   +3   +4   +5   +6   +7
3 → 5 → 8 → 12 → 17 → 23 → 30

b
+3   +5   +7   +9   +11   +13   +15
3 → 6 → 11 → 18 → 27 → 38 → 51 → 66

A2 a 10th number is 30 + 8 + 9 + 10 = 57
       The 10th number is the 9th number plus 10.
    b 10th number is 66 + 17 + 19 = 102
       The 10th number is the 9th number plus (2 × 10 − 1)

A3 Children grow their own shape starting with 5 counters.

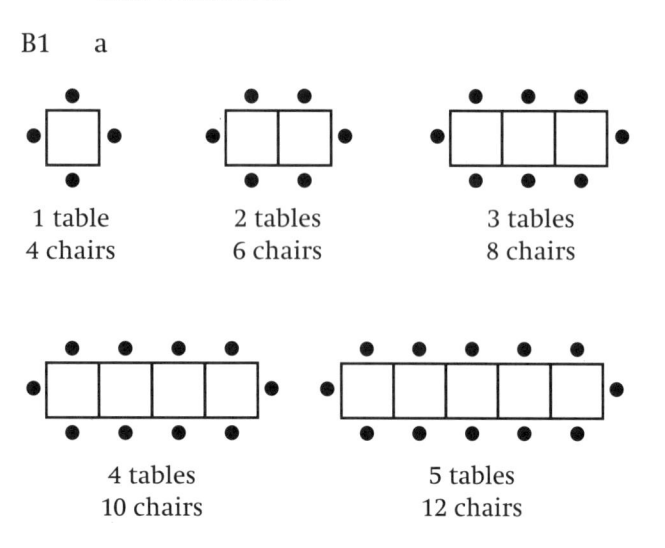

B1 a

1 table   2 tables   3 tables
4 chairs   6 chairs   8 chairs

4 tables   5 tables
10 chairs   12 chairs

For any number of tables, there are twice that number of chairs plus 2 more.

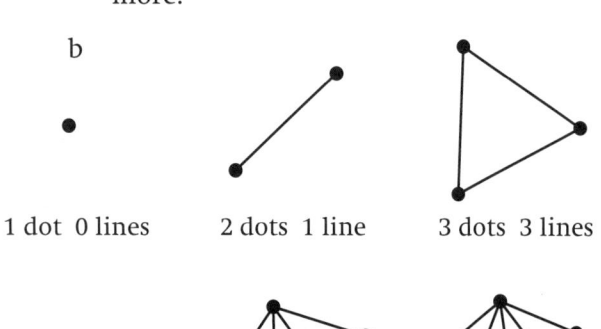

b

1 dot 0 lines   2 dots 1 line   3 dots 3 lines

The number of dots goes up one each time. The number of lines is the sequence of triangular numbers, starting with 0. If n is the number of dots, the number of lines is the $(n − 1)$th triangular number.

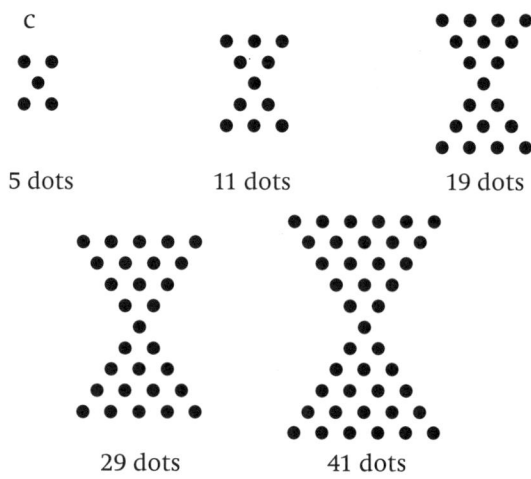

c

5 dots   11 dots   19 dots

29 dots   41 dots

The number of dots in any diagram is twice the next triangular number less 1. The pattern is 5 (+6) 11 (+8) 19 (+10) 29 (+12) 41 (+14)

B2 a

1	2	5	10	17	26	37	50
4	3	6	11	18	27	38	
9	8	7	12	19	28	39	
16	15	14	13	20	29	40	
25	24	23	22	21	30	41	
36	35	34	33	32	31	42	
49	48	47	46	45	44	43	

b The numbers in the 1st column are square numbers.

c The square numbers will all be in the 1st column.

The number of squares in a square is a square number. Each number in the 1st column is the number of squares in the square with one corner at top left and another the numbered square.

C1 a

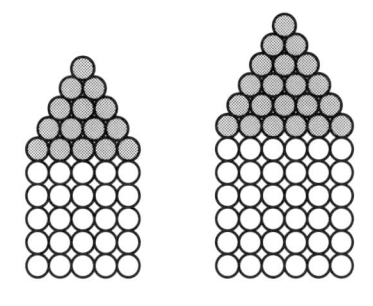

b There are 100 + 55 = 155 counters in the 10th shape.
c The 10th shape is made of the 10th square number and the sum of the first 10 counting numbers.

C2 Children design their own shape and grow it.

Homework suggestion

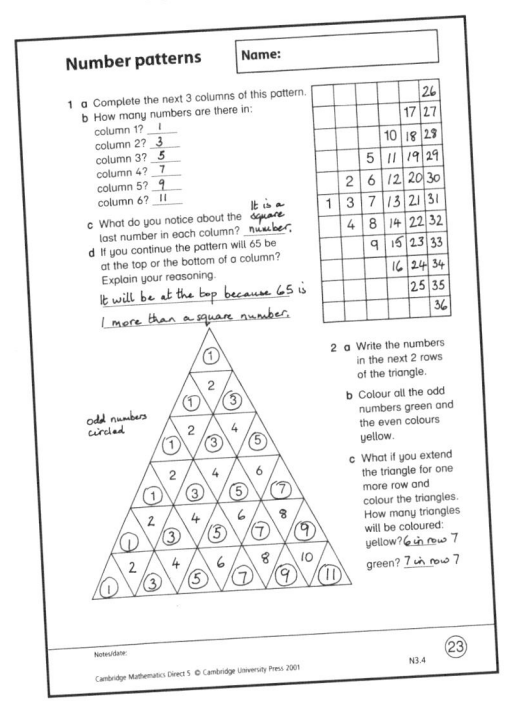

CM 25

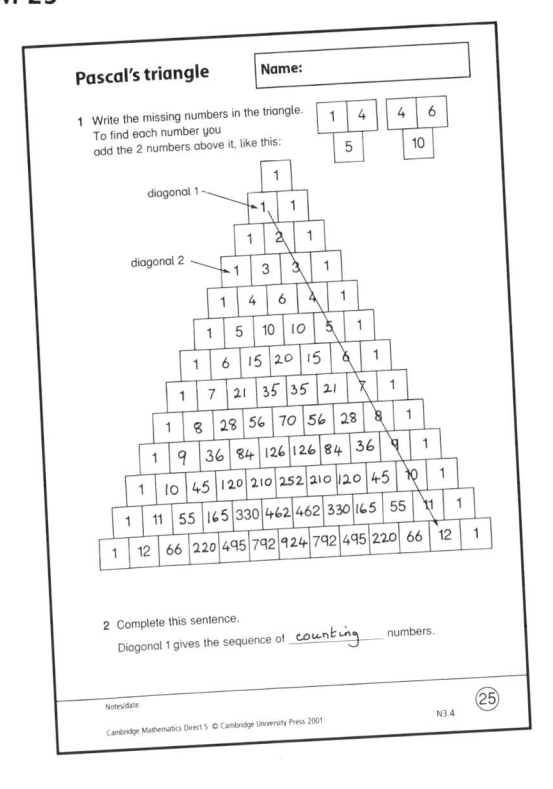

N3.5 Finding and using the rule

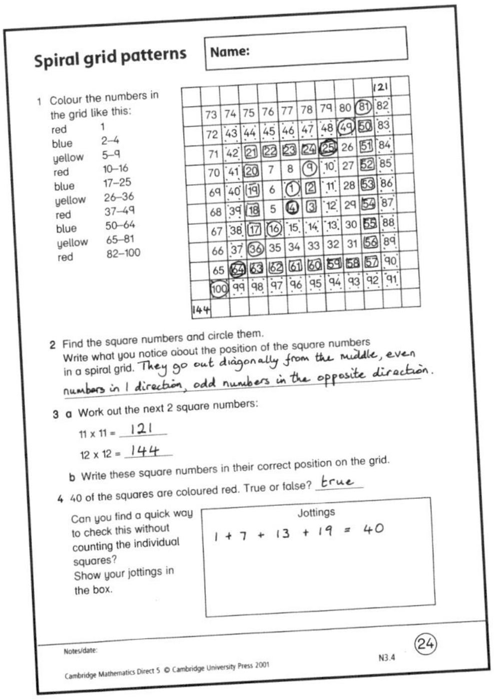

TB pages 42–43

A1   b, c

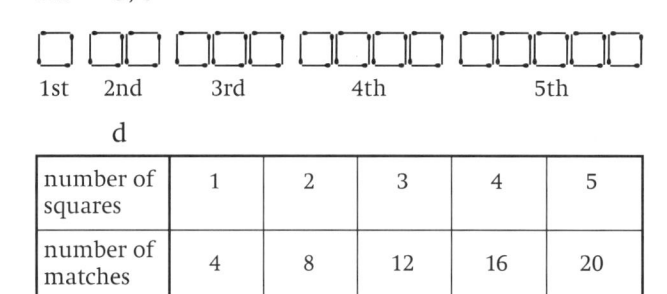

1st   2nd   3rd   4th   5th

d

number of squares	1	2	3	4	5
number of matches	4	8	12	16	20

e You need 4 more matches for the next pattern each time. (The number of matches is 4 times the number of squares.)

A2   a

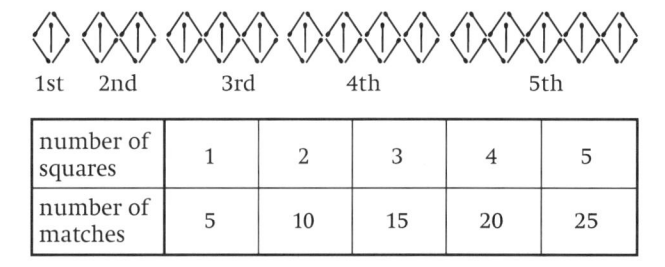

1st   2nd   3rd   4th   5th

number of squares	1	2	3	4	5
number of matches	5	10	15	20	25

The number of matches increases by 5 each time. (The number of matches is 5 times the number of squares.)

B1 a

number of squares	1	2	3	4	5	6	7	8
number of matches	4	7	10	13	16	19	22	25

The number of matches is 3 times the number of squares, plus 1.

b

number of squares	1	2	3	4	5	6	7	8
number of matches	6	11	16	21	26	31	36	41

The number of matches is 5 times the number of squares, plus 1.

B2

number of shapes	1	2	3	4	....	10	....	20
number of matches	5	9	13	17		41		81

The number of matches is 4 times the number of shapes, then add 1.

C1

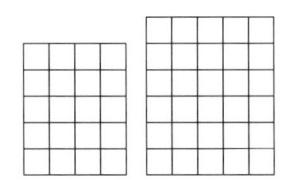

10th diagram

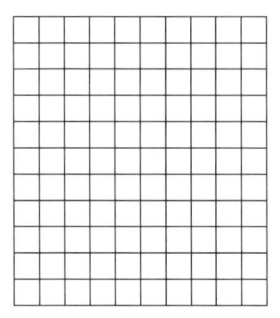

The number of squares is 10 times (10 + 1), or 10 times 11.

Fractions, decimals and percentages, ratio and proportion

F1.1 Equivalent fractions

TB pages 44–45

A1

A2 a $\frac{1}{2} = \frac{2}{4}$ b $\frac{1}{2} = \frac{3}{6}$
    c $\frac{1}{2} = \frac{4}{8}$ d $\frac{1}{2} = \frac{5}{10}$
    e $\frac{1}{2} = \frac{6}{12}$ f $\frac{1}{2} = \frac{8}{16}$

A3 a The numerator is half the denominator. The denominator is always twice as big as the numerator.
    b $\frac{1}{2} = \frac{7}{14}$
    c $\frac{1}{2} = \frac{9}{18}$
    d The numerator had to be half the size of the denominator.

A4 For example, $\frac{1}{2} = \frac{10}{20}$, $\frac{1}{2} = \frac{12}{24}$, $\frac{1}{2} = \frac{50}{100}$

B1

B2 a $\frac{1}{4} = \frac{2}{8}$ b $\frac{1}{4} = \frac{3}{12}$ c $\frac{1}{4} = \frac{4}{16}$
    d $\frac{1}{4} = \frac{5}{20}$ e $\frac{1}{4} = \frac{6}{24}$ f $\frac{1}{4} = \frac{7}{28}$

B3 a The numerator is quarter the denominator. The denominator is always 4 times as big as the numerator.
    b $\frac{1}{4} = \frac{8}{32}$ c $\frac{1}{4} = \frac{9}{36}$

d The numerator had to be a quarter the size of the denominator.

B4 For example, $\frac{1}{4} = \frac{10}{40}$, $\frac{1}{4} = \frac{20}{80}$, $\frac{1}{4} = \frac{25}{100}$

C1 Fraction game

F1.2 Thirds, sixths, ninths

TB pages 46–47

A1

[fraction wall showing $\frac{1}{3}$, $\frac{1}{6}$, $\frac{1}{9}$, $\frac{1}{12}$, $\frac{1}{15}$, $\frac{1}{18}$, $\frac{1}{21}$, $\frac{1}{24}$, $\frac{1}{27}$]

A2 a $\frac{1}{3} = \frac{2}{6}$ b $\frac{1}{3} = \frac{3}{9}$
    c $\frac{1}{3} = \frac{4}{12}$ d $\frac{1}{3} = \frac{5}{15}$
    e $\frac{1}{3} = \frac{6}{18}$ f $\frac{1}{3} = \frac{7}{21}$
    g $\frac{1}{3} = \frac{8}{24}$ h $\frac{1}{3} = \frac{9}{27}$
    i $\frac{1}{3} = \frac{10}{30}$

A3 For example: $\frac{1}{3} = \frac{11}{33}$, $\frac{1}{3} = \frac{12}{36}$, $\frac{1}{3} = \frac{20}{60}$

B1 [number line from 0 to 1 marked $\frac{1}{6}$, $\frac{1}{3}$, $\frac{1}{2}$, $\frac{2}{3}$, $\frac{5}{6}$]

B2 a One sixth is a half of **one third**.
    b Three sixths are a half of **one whole**.
    c Two **sixths** are one third of a whole.
    d Three ninths are one **third** of a whole.
    e Four **twelfths** are one third of a whole.

B3 a $\frac{1}{2}, \frac{1}{6}, \frac{1}{9}$ b $\frac{1}{4}, \frac{1}{6}, \frac{1}{12}$

C1 1 and 5, 2 and 6, 3 and 7, 4 and 8, 5 and 9, 6 and 10, 7 and 11, 8 and 12, 9 and 1, 10 and 2, 11 and 3, 12 and 4

C2 1 and 3, 2 and 4, 3 and 5, 4 and 6, 5 and 7, 6 and 8, 7 and 9, 8 and 10, 9 and 11, 10 and 12, 11 and 1, 12 and 2

C3 1 and 2, 2 and 3, 3 and 4, 4 and 5, 5 and 6, 6 and 7, 7 and 8, 8 and 9, 9 and 10, 10 and 11, 11 and 12, 12 and 1

Homework suggestion

For example:

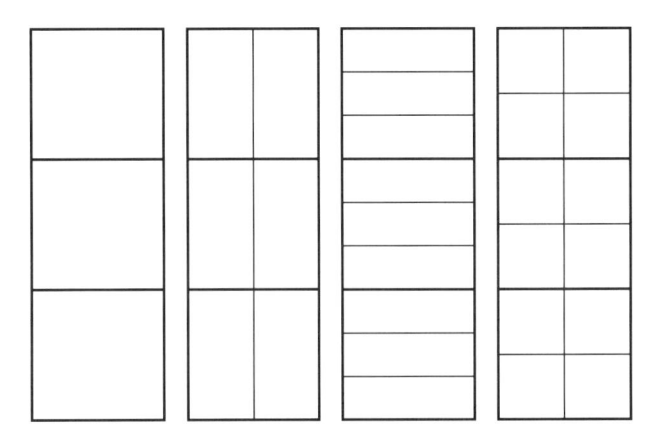

[four rectangular grids divided into different numbers of parts]

F1.4 Tenths and hundredths

TB pages 48–50

★1 a $\frac{3}{10}$ or 0.3   b $\frac{6}{10}$ or 0.6
    c $\frac{1}{10}$ or 0.1   d $\frac{9}{10}$ or 0.9

A1 a 0.9   b 0.3
    c 0.1   d 0.7
    e 0.5   f 0.6
    g 0.8

A2 a $\frac{4}{10}$ or 0.4   b $\frac{5}{10}$ or 0.5
    c $\frac{7}{10}$ or 0.7   d $\frac{1}{10}$ or 0.1

A3 a 0.5 or $\frac{5}{10}$ b 0.2 or $\frac{2}{10}$
    c 0.8 or $\frac{8}{10}$ d 0.6 or $\frac{6}{10}$
    e 0.3 or $\frac{3}{10}$

B1 [number line from 0 to 1 marked $\frac{10}{100}$, $\frac{20}{100}$, $\frac{30}{100}$, $\frac{40}{100}$, $\frac{50}{100}$, $\frac{60}{100}$, $\frac{70}{100}$, $\frac{80}{100}$, $\frac{90}{100}$]

B2 $\frac{2}{100}, \frac{9}{100}, \frac{4}{10}, \frac{1}{2}, \frac{51}{100}, \frac{6}{10}, \frac{73}{100}, \frac{3}{4}$

B3 Paired activity

C1 Fraction pelmanism

F1.5 Improper fractions

TB pages 51–53

★1 a $1\frac{1}{2}$ b $\frac{3}{2}$
    c $2\frac{1}{4}$ d $\frac{9}{4}$

★2 a $2\frac{5}{6}$ b $3\frac{3}{4}$

A1 a $\frac{5}{3}$ or $1\frac{2}{3}$ b $\frac{7}{3}$ or $2\frac{1}{3}$

A2 a $\frac{13}{8}$ or $1\frac{5}{8}$ b $\frac{23}{10}$ or $2\frac{3}{10}$

A3 a $\frac{11}{6}$ or $1\frac{5}{6}$ b $\frac{25}{10}$ or $2\frac{5}{10}$ or $2\frac{1}{2}$

B1 Children's illustrations. The whole can be any shape as long as it is divided into the correct number of equal parts, e.g.

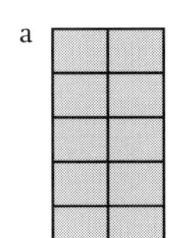

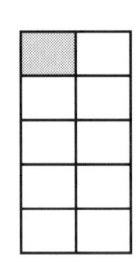

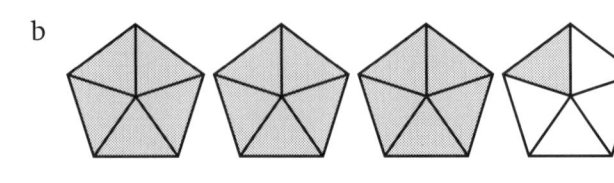

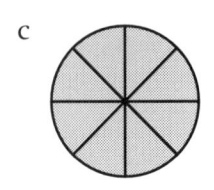

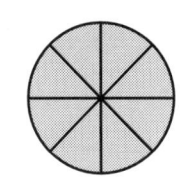

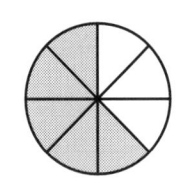

a

b

c

B2 a $1\frac{7}{10}$ b $1\frac{5}{8}$ c $4\frac{1}{5}$
    d $3\frac{1}{2}$ e $6\frac{1}{4}$ f $5\frac{1}{3}$

B3 a $\frac{8}{5}$ b $\frac{5}{2}$ c $\frac{7}{6}$
    d $\frac{7}{4}$ e $\frac{51}{5}$ f $\frac{29}{9}$

C1 $2\frac{1}{3}$

C2 $7\frac{1}{4}$

C3 $3\frac{2}{5}$

C4 $16\frac{1}{2}$ kg

C5 $3\frac{1}{5}$ km

F2.1 Introducing hundredths

TB page 54

B1 a 7.51 = 7 + **0.5** + **0.01**
    b 3.24 = 3 + 0.2 + **0.04**
    c 8.09 = 8 + **0.09**   or   8.09 = 8 + 0.0 + **0.09**
    d 11.64 = 10 + 1 + **0.6** + **0.04**

B2 a 0.3   b 6.7   c 1.4   d 0.04
    e 0.35 f 0.62 g 1.82 h 5.09

B3 a $\frac{4}{10}$ b $8\frac{1}{10}$ or $\frac{81}{10}$
    c $\frac{43}{100}$ d $\frac{7}{100}$
    e $\frac{2}{100}$ f $3\frac{6}{100}$ or $\frac{306}{100}$
    g $1\frac{52}{100}$ or $\frac{152}{100}$ h $\frac{79}{100}$

C1 For example:
    a 4.73 = 4 units + 7 tenths + 3 hundredths
    b 4.37, 3.74, 3.47, 7.34, 7.43

C2 Repeat of C1 for 3 other choices of cards

F2.2 Ordering decimals

TB pages 55–56

★1 CM 37

A1 CM 37

A2 3.11, 4.04, 4.31, 5.72, 6.82, 7.29, 8.63, 9.45

A3 9.64 m, 8.59 m, 7.59 m, 6.24 m, 5.39 m, 4.86 m, 3.41 m, 1.87 m

B1 a 4.11, 4.12, 4.13, 4.14, 4.15, 4.16
    b 9.78, 9.79, 9.8, 9.81, 9.82, 9.83, 9.84, 9.85, 9.86, 9.87
    c 3.46, 3.45, 3.44, 3.43, 3.42, 3.41
    d 6.91, 6.92, 6.93, 6.94, 6.95, 6.96, 6.97, 6.98, 6.99
    e 5.71. 5.7, 5.69, 5.68, 5.67, 5.66, 5.65, 5.64, 5.63
    f 8.01, 8.02, 8.03, 8.04, 8.05, 8.06, 8.07, 8.08, 8.09, 8.1, 8.11, 8.12

B2 a 7.9, **8.1**, 8.3, 8.5, **8.7**, 8.9
    b 5.6, 5.9, **6.2**, **6.5**, 6.8, 7.1
    c 8.3, **8.0**, 7.7, 7.4, **7.1**, 6.8
    d 3.9, 3.4, **2.9**, **2.4**, 1.9, 1.4

C1 Children's own trail with difference of 0.01

C2 Children's own trail with difference of 0.03

CM 37

1 8.4, 8.5, 8.6, 8.7, 8.8, 8.9, 9, 9.1, 9.2

2 9.8, 9.7, 9.6, 9.5, 9.4, 9.3, 9.2, 9.1

3 2.6, 2.7, 2.8, 2.9, 3, 3.1, 3.2

4 6.9, 6.8, 6.7, 6.6, 6.5, 6.4, 6.3

5 5.9, 5.8, 5.7, 5.6, 5.5, 5.4, 5.3

6 4.1, 4, 3.9, 3.8, 3.7, 3.6, 3.5

7 2.7, 2.6, 2.5, 2.4, 2.3, 2.2, 2.1, 2, 1.9

8 0.6, 0.7, 0.8, 0.9, 1, 1.1, 1.2

9 0.1, 0.2, 0.3, 0.4, 0.5, 0.6, 0.7, 0.8, 0.9, 1, 1.1

F2.4 Changing units

TB pages 57–58

A1   4.2 kg or 4200 g

A2   7.9 m or 790 cm

A3   5.8 m or 580 cm

B1   8500 g

B2   10.2 m or 1020 cm

B3   54 paper clips

B4   13 tiles

B5   6 kg

C1   Children's own problems using mixed units

F3.1 Finding equivalents

TB page 59

1 a 0.3   b 0.9   c 0.5
   d 0.02   e 0.46   f 0.99
   g 0.8   h 0.8 or 0.80   i 0.75
   j 0.1 or 0.01 k 0.6   l 0.04

2 a $\frac{9}{10}$ b $\frac{3}{100}$ c $\frac{52}{100}$
   d $\frac{25}{100}$ e $\frac{66}{100}$ f $\frac{7}{100}$
   g $\frac{7}{10}$ h $\frac{11}{100}$ i $\frac{1}{100}$
   j $\frac{35}{100}$ k $\frac{5}{100}$ l $\frac{6}{10}$

3 Children's own examples

F3.2 Calculator fractions

TB page 60

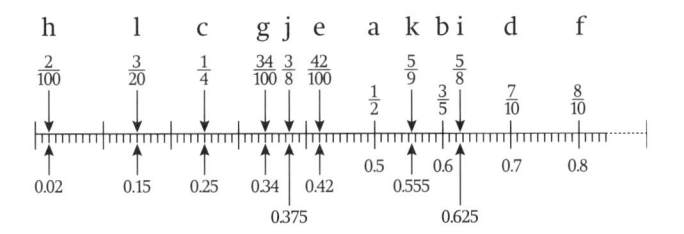

```
h         l        c        g  j     e        a     k b i     d         f
2/100   3/20     1/4    34/100 3/8  42/100   5/9   3/5  7/10  8/10
                                     1/2          5/8
 ↓        ↓       ↓       ↓  ↓      ↓        ↓    ↓  ↓ ↓      ↓        ↓
|---------|-------|-------|--|------|--------|----|--|-|------|--------|
0.02    0.15    0.25    0.34  0.42                 0.7       0.8
                           0.375   0.5    0.6
                                      0.555
                                            0.625
```

F3.3 Decimals for money and length

TB pages 61–62

A1 a 29 cm = 0.29 m   b 50p = £0.50
    c 133p = £1.33   d 105 cm = 1.05 m
    e 8p = £0.08   f 7 cm = 0.07 m
    g 220 cm = 2.2 m   h 425p = £4.25
    i 10p = £0.10   j 75 cm = 0.75 m
    k 111p = £1.11   l 60 cm = 0.6 m

A2 CM 44

B1 a £1.25 = 125p or £1 and 25p
    b £0.03 = 3p
    c 1.43 m = 143 cm
    d 0.25 m = 25 cm
    e £0.84 = 84p
    f 0.71 m = 71 cm
    g £2.02 = 202p or £2 and 2p
    h 3.11 m = 311 cm
    i £0.10 = 10p
    j 1.52 m = 152 cm
    k £5.55 = 555p or £5 and 55p
    l 0.49 m = 49 cm

B2 a 308p or £3.08
    b 433p or £4.33
    c 597p or £5.97

C1 a cheese roll, cranberry crush and sherbert shimmies cost £3.95, with 5p change
       salad sandwich, yummy yogurts and choco chums cost £3.97, with 3p change
       salad sandwich, jam tarts and crusty crumbs cost £3.98, with 2p change
       cheese roll and 2 packs of jam tarts cost £3.99, with 1p change
    b cheese roll and 2 packs of sherbert shimmies cost £1.29, with £2.71 change
       cheese roll, sherbert shimmies and bacon bites cost £1.73, with £2.27 change

CM 45

100p → £1.00

£0.25 → 25p

25 cm → 0.25 m

0.1 m → 10 cm

0.4 m → 40 cm

40p → £0.40

75p → £0.75

£2.50 → 250p

0.39 m → 39 cm

1 m → 100 cm

F4.1 Comparing fractions

TB page 63

A1 a $\frac{1}{4} > \frac{1}{6}$ b $\frac{1}{9} < \frac{1}{8}$
    c $\frac{1}{5} < \frac{1}{2}$ d $\frac{1}{3} > \frac{1}{6}$
    e $\frac{1}{4} < \frac{1}{3}$ f $\frac{1}{6} < \frac{1}{2}$
    g $\frac{1}{10} < \frac{1}{6}$ h $\frac{1}{8} > \frac{1}{10}$
    i $\frac{1}{4} < \frac{1}{3}$ j $\frac{1}{6} > \frac{1}{8}$

B1 10 of: $\frac{4}{5} > \frac{3}{4}$ $\frac{4}{5} > \frac{2}{3}$
$\frac{4}{5} > \frac{1}{2}$ $\frac{4}{5} > \frac{3}{8}$
$\frac{4}{5} > \frac{1}{6}$ $\frac{3}{4} > \frac{2}{3}$
$\frac{3}{4} > \frac{1}{2}$ $\frac{3}{4} > \frac{3}{8}$
$\frac{3}{4} > \frac{1}{6}$ $\frac{2}{3} > \frac{1}{2}$
$\frac{2}{3} > \frac{3}{8}$ $\frac{2}{3} > \frac{1}{6}$
$\frac{1}{2} > \frac{3}{8}$ $\frac{1}{2} > \frac{1}{6}$
$\frac{3}{8} > \frac{1}{6}$

Each of these statements can be written in reverse order using the < sign, for example $\frac{3}{4} < \frac{4}{5}$.

C1 Game using cards from CM 48
The fraction are, from smallest to largest:
$\frac{1}{10} < \frac{1}{9} < \frac{1}{8} < \frac{1}{6} < \frac{1}{5} = \frac{2}{10} < \frac{2}{9} < \frac{1}{4} = \frac{2}{8} < \frac{1}{3} = \frac{2}{6} = \frac{3}{9} < \frac{2}{5}$
$< \frac{1}{2} = \frac{2}{4} = \frac{4}{8} = \frac{3}{6} < \frac{5}{9} < \frac{5}{8} < \frac{2}{3} = \frac{6}{9} < \frac{3}{4} < \frac{4}{5} < \frac{5}{6} < \frac{7}{8}$

C2 Children's own game using the fraction cards

F4.2 Ordering fractions

TB page 64

B1 a $\frac{1}{4} < \frac{5}{12}$ b $\frac{8}{8} = 1$
c $1 > \frac{8}{9}$ d $\frac{6}{8} = \frac{3}{4}$
e $\frac{9}{8} > 1$ f $\frac{5}{20} < \frac{6}{10}$
g $1\frac{3}{4} > \frac{15}{10}$ h $\frac{2}{10} = \frac{1}{5}$
i $1\frac{1}{4} < 1\frac{2}{3}$ j $\frac{11}{10} < 1\frac{1}{2}$
k $\frac{7}{10} > \frac{1}{2}$ l $\frac{4}{9} > \frac{1}{4}$

B2 a $\frac{1}{2} < 1 < 1\frac{1}{4}$ b $\frac{15}{12} < 1\frac{1}{2} < \frac{9}{4}$

C1 For example:
a $\frac{1}{8} < \frac{1}{7}$ or $\frac{1}{6}$ or $\frac{1}{5}$ or $\frac{1}{4}$ or $\frac{1}{3} < \frac{1}{2}$
b $\frac{1}{2} < \frac{2}{3}$ or $\frac{3}{4}$ or 1 or $1\frac{1}{4}$ or $1\frac{1}{2} < 1\frac{3}{4}$
c $\frac{1}{2} < \frac{5}{9}$ or $\frac{5}{8}$ or $\frac{5}{7}$ or $\frac{2}{3} < \frac{3}{4}$
d $\frac{8}{9} > \frac{7}{9} > \frac{2}{3}$

C2 Children's 3 number sentences

F4.3 Ordering decimals

TB page 65

A1 a 0.1, 0.3, 0.5, 0.8, 0.9
b 0.25, 0.5, 0.55, 0.75
c 0.5, 1.0, 1.5, 2.0, 2.5
d 1.5, 1.75, 2.25, 2.75, 3.00
e 0.35, 3.05, 3.50, 5.03, 5.30

A2 Children's 3 lists of 5 numbers, starting with the largest number

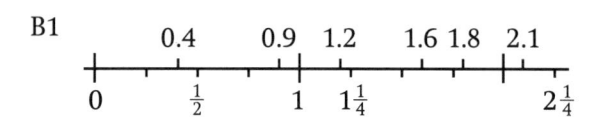

B1 (number line: 0.4, 0.9, 1.2, 1.6, 1.8, 2.1 marked on a line from 0 to $2\frac{1}{4}$ with $\frac{1}{2}$, 1, $1\frac{1}{4}$ labelled)

B2 (number line: $5\frac{1}{10}$, $5\frac{1}{4}$, $6\frac{3}{6}$, $6\frac{2}{3}$, $7\frac{1}{8}$ marked on a line from 5 to 7.5 with 5.2, 5.6, 6.1, 6.5 labelled)

C1 a 4.6, $1\frac{1}{4}$, $\frac{15}{30}$, $\frac{7}{15}$, 0.3, $\frac{1}{8}$
b $\frac{9}{4}$, 1.9, $\frac{7}{8}$, $\frac{10}{12}$, 0.5, 0.2
c $\frac{20}{2}$, $6\frac{3}{4}$, 5.8, 4.8, 3.1, $\frac{6}{3}$

C2 Children's 2 lists 6 numbers, starting with the lowest number

CM 53

$0.75 \rightarrow \frac{3}{4}$
$0.6 \rightarrow \frac{6}{10}$
$0.8 \rightarrow \frac{8}{10}$
$0.21 \rightarrow \frac{21}{100}$
$0.5 \rightarrow \frac{1}{2}$
$0.1 \rightarrow \frac{1}{10}$
$0.1 \rightarrow \frac{10}{100}$
$0.25 \rightarrow \frac{1}{4}$
$0.01 \rightarrow \frac{1}{100}$
$0.8 \rightarrow \frac{80}{100}$

F5.1 Fractions and division 1

TB pages 66–67

A1 a 6   b 5   c 2
d 5   e 6   f £1

A2 a 10 cm   b 25 cm
c 10p   d 1p

A3 a 18   b 10   c 10
d 10   e 15   f 15

A4 a 30p   b 70 cm
c 19p   80 cm

C1 a 96 cm   b £200   c 80 cm
d 2 m 40 cm   e £217   f 40 cm

C2 a, b $\frac{1}{2}$ of 24 = 12 (also $\frac{2}{4}, \frac{3}{6}, \frac{4}{8}, \frac{6}{12}$)
$\frac{1}{3}$ of 24 = 8 (also $\frac{2}{6}, \frac{4}{12}$)
$\frac{2}{3}$ of 24 = 16 (also $\frac{4}{6}, \frac{8}{12}$)
$\frac{1}{4}$ of 24 = 6 (also $\frac{2}{8}, \frac{3}{12}$)
$\frac{3}{4}$ of 24 = 18 (also $\frac{6}{8}, \frac{9}{12}$)
$\frac{1}{6}$ of 24 = 4 (also $\frac{2}{12}$)
$\frac{5}{6}$ of 24 = 20 (also $\frac{10}{12}$)
$\frac{1}{8}$ of 24 = 3
$\frac{3}{8}$ of 24 = 9
$\frac{5}{8}$ of 24 = 15
$\frac{7}{8}$ of 24 = 21
$\frac{1}{12}$ of 24 = 2
$\frac{5}{12}$ of 24 = 10
$\frac{7}{12}$ of 24 = 14
$\frac{11}{12}$ of 24 = 22

c   Children find fractions of a number of their own choice. For example 36 gives more fractions.

CM 55

$\frac{1}{3}$ of 9 3	$\frac{1}{10}$ of 100 10	$\frac{1}{5}$ of £25 £5
$\frac{1}{8}$ of 24 3	$\frac{1}{6}$ of 18 m 3 m	$\frac{1}{3}$ of £30 £10
$\frac{1}{5}$ of 35 7	$\frac{1}{5}$ of 15 3	$\frac{1}{7}$ of 14 2
$\frac{1}{4}$ of £40 £10	$\frac{1}{3}$ of 21 7	$\frac{1}{8}$ of 40 5
$\frac{1}{10}$ of £1 10p	$\frac{1}{10}$ of 50 5	$\frac{1}{10}$ of 500 50
$\frac{1}{5}$ of 1 m 20 cm	$\frac{1}{4}$ of 16 4	$\frac{1}{9}$ of £45 £5

Fractions of numbers 1
Cambridge Mathematics Direct 5 © Cambridge University Press 2001   F5.1   55

CM56

$\frac{2}{3}$ of 9 6	$\frac{3}{10}$ of 100 30	$\frac{2}{5}$ of £25 £10
$\frac{3}{8}$ of 24 9	$\frac{5}{6}$ of 18 15	$\frac{2}{3}$ of £30 £20
$\frac{3}{5}$ of 35 21	$\frac{4}{5}$ of 15 12	$\frac{3}{7}$ of 14 6
$\frac{3}{4}$ of £40 £30	$\frac{2}{3}$ of 21 14	$\frac{3}{8}$ of 40 15
$\frac{7}{10}$ of £10 £7	$\frac{9}{10}$ of 50 45	$\frac{4}{10}$ of £500 £200
$\frac{7}{9}$ of £45 £35	$\frac{3}{4}$ of 16 12	$\frac{4}{5}$ of 1 m 80 cm

Fractions of numbers 2
Cambridge Mathematics Direct 5 © Cambridge University Press 2001   F5.1   56

F5.2 Fractions and division 2

TB pages 68–69

A1 a $\frac{1}{5}$ b $\frac{2}{3}$

A2 a $\frac{15}{3}$ b $\frac{20}{5}$ c $\frac{16}{8}$

A3 a $\frac{3}{10}$ b $\frac{7}{10}$

A4 a $\frac{2}{8}$ or $\frac{1}{4}$ b $\frac{6}{8}$ or $\frac{3}{4}$

B1 a $\frac{3}{10}$ b $\frac{4}{7}$

B2 a $18 \div 6 = 3$ b $24 \div 8 = 3$ c $35 \div 5 = 7$
    d $\frac{32}{4} = 8$ e $\frac{36}{9} = 4$ f $\frac{42}{7} = 6$

B3 a $\frac{1}{24}$ b $\frac{6}{24}$ or $\frac{1}{4}$ c $\frac{11}{24}$

B4 a $\frac{1}{4}$ or $\frac{3}{12}$ b $\frac{4}{1}$ or $\frac{12}{3}$

F5.3 Problems involving proportion

TB pages 70–71

A1 a 12 tokens   b 4 bags

A2 a 2 in every 3 squares are white.
    b For example:

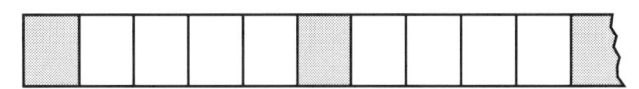

    c 4 in every 5 squares are white.
    d 12 white squares
    e 4 red squares

B1 a
Tins bought	Free tins	Total of tins
3	1	4
6	2	8
15	5	20
30	10	40

    b 1 in every 4 tins is free.
       You pay for 3 times as many tins as you get free.

B2 a 8 oranges make 1 litre of juice.
    b She needs 16 oranges for 2 litres of juice.

B3 a 3 fish   b 8 fish

C1 a 25 girls   b 45 children
    c 16 boys   d 36 children

C2 a Children's triangle patterns with 4 white triangles for every 1 black
    b 3 out of:
       For every black triangle there are 4 white triangles.
       For every 4 white triangles there is 1 black triangle.

In every 5 triangles there is 1 black triangle.
In every 5 triangles there are 4 white triangles.
There are 4 times as many white triangles as black
There are a quarter as many black triangles as white.

F5.4 Quotients and fractions

TB page 72

A1 a $6\frac{1}{2}$ b $8\frac{1}{2}$
    c $3\frac{2}{3}$ d $4\frac{2}{3}$
    e $4\frac{2}{4}$ or $4\frac{1}{2}$ f $5\frac{1}{4}$
    g $5\frac{3}{5}$ h $6\frac{2}{5}$

B1 a $9\frac{1}{4}$ b $5\frac{5}{6}$
    c $9\frac{4}{6}$ or $9\frac{2}{3}$ d $2\frac{5}{7}$
    e $2\frac{6}{9}$ or $2\frac{2}{3}$ f $5\frac{3}{9}$ or $5\frac{1}{3}$
    g $4\frac{2}{10}$ or $4\frac{1}{5}$ h $9\frac{9}{10}$

C1 a $8\frac{4}{7}$ b $3\frac{7}{8}$
    c $9\frac{4}{9}$ d $7\frac{3}{7}$
    e $8\frac{6}{8}$ or $8\frac{3}{4}$ f $5\frac{6}{8}$ or $5\frac{3}{4}$
    g $6\frac{5}{7}$ h $6\frac{4}{9}$

C2 a $15 \div 4$ b $25 \div 9$ c $3 \div 10$
    Other answers are possible.

F5.5 Quotients and decimals

TB page 73

A1 a 7.5 b 10.5 c 3.25
    d 2.75 e 9.5 f 3.1

A2 a 15 b 23 c 38
    d 8 e 18 f 4

B1 a 9.25 b 7.2 c 10.75
    d 9.6 e 8.2 f 9.5

B2 a 20 b 31 c 26
    d 71 e 11 f 82

B3 a $10.25 \approx 10$ b $9.75 \approx 10$ c $5.8 \approx 6$

CM 59

$41 \div 4 = 10.25$ $23 \div 4 = 5.75$ $57 \div 10 = 5.7$
$29 \div 5 = 5.8$ $36 \div 5 = 7.2$ $53 \div 5 = 10.6$
$30 \div 4 = 7.5$ $63 \div 10 = 6.3$ $33 \div 5 = 6.6$
$13 \div 2 = 6.5$

F6.1 Introducing percentages

TB page 74

A1 a red 50%, yellow 40%, blue 10%
    b yellow 40%, green 40%, blue 20%
    c green 60%, blue 10%, grey 10%, purple 10%, red 10%

B1 a $\frac{1}{2}$ = **50%** red
    b 10% yellow = $\frac{1}{10}$ yellow
    c 25% blue = $\frac{1}{4}$ blue
    d 100% green = **all** green

B2 Children create their own carpet on CM 60 that is 25% yellow, 10% green, 25% blue, 40% white

C1
carpet	red	blue	yellow	green
a	$\frac{1}{2}$	**35%**	**10%**	**5%**
b	**40%**	**10%**	$\frac{1}{4}$	**25%**
c	**10%**	**80%**	0	$\frac{1}{10}$
d	**15%**	$\frac{1}{4}$	**50%**	**10%**

F6.2 Percentages of a shape

TB pages 75–76

★1 a $\frac{1}{2}$ ($\frac{4}{8}$, $\frac{6}{12}$, ... $\frac{50}{100}$ would also be correct)
    b $\frac{1}{4}$ ($\frac{4}{16}$, $\frac{6}{24}$, ... $\frac{25}{100}$ would also be correct)
    c $\frac{1}{2}$ ($\frac{10}{20}$, ... $\frac{50}{100}$ would also be correct)
    d $\frac{1}{4}$ ($\frac{6}{24}$, ... would also be correct)
    e $\frac{1}{10}$ ($\frac{4}{40}$, ... would also be correct)

★2 a 50% b 25% c 50%
    d 25% e 10%

A1 a brown 50%, black 50%
    b orange, yellow, brown and pink 25% each
    c black 50%, white 50%
    d white 50%, green 25%, blue 25%

A2 a red 50%, white 50%
    b red, white, blue, yellow 25% each

B1 Children colour the diagrams on CM 61:
    a 25% red, 25% yellow, 50% blue
    b brown, yellow, blue, white, 25% each
    c 25% orange, 25% blue, 10% each yellow, white, red, green and black

C1 Children colour the diagrams on CM 62, and state the percentage and fraction of each colour.